THIS BOOK BELONGS TO...*

AND IT'S GNASHER PROTECTED!

WHITE PAINT

DENNIS & GNASHER

THE WORLD'S WILDEST BOY... AND HIS BEST FRIEND!

TIME TO GET UP, LIGHT OF MY LIFE.

URRGH!

COFFEE!

GRASP!

GRASP!

I'LL LEAVE IT HERE. DRINKING COFFEE UNDER THE COVERS DOESN'T END WELL, IF YOU REMEMBER.

THE TELLY SAYS IT'S THE FIRST DAY OF SPRING!

AH! LOOK AT THAT! WE MADE IT THROUGH ANOTHER UNFORGIVING WINTER!

I'LL SHOW YOU UNFORGIVING IF YOU DON'T CLOSE THOSE CURTAINS!

DOWNSTAIRS...

WHAT DO YOU THINK OF THE NEW LOOK, GNASHER?

SAME AS THE OLD LOOK?

THIS IS MY **SPRING** JUMPER. IT'S SLIGHTLY THINNER THAN MY WINTER ONE, BUT THICKER THAN MY SUMMER JUMPER.

OF COURSE!

COME ON! LET'S GET OUT THERE!

AS LONG AS WE DON'T DO ANYTHING STUPID!

NO-ONE WOULD HAVE BELIEVED THAT DENNIS'S MOVEMENTS WERE BEING WATCHED. HE WAS BEING STUDIED LIKE SOMEONE WITH A MICROSCOPE WATCHES THOSE LITTLE BUGS IN DIRTY WATER. NO-ONE CONSIDERED THE POSSIBILITY OF SOMEONE GETTING BACK AT DENNIS FOR THAT THING HE DID THAT TIME. AND YET, A MIND LOADS BETTER THAN DENNIS'S WATCHED AND SLOWLY, SURELY DREW UP PLANS AGAINST HIM.

THE BASH STREET KIDS

THE CLASS EVERY TEACHER DREADS...

BAH! THE FIRST DAY OF THE SPRING TERM ALREADY!

YEAH...

CRUNCH! MUNCH!

...I WONDER WHAT OUR PROJECT IS GOING TO BE?

CRISPS

PONK!

I SUPPOSE WE SHOULD GET TO CLASS AND FIND OUT!

HEY!

TOSS!

JANITOR, WHAT'S WRONG?

I CAN'T TAKE IT ANY MORE! THE KIDS TREAT THIS SCHOOL LIKE A PIGSTY!

HUH! WE DO NOT!

CRISPS

SNAP!

SNAP!

COMING THROUGH!

THUMP!

BUMP!

THUNDER OF HOOVES!

THEN AGAIN...

DON'T WORRY, JANITOR! I'VE AN IDEA THAT WILL PUT THE SPRING BACK IN YOUR STEP!

WHY DON'T I LIKE THE SOUND OF THAT?

IN CLASS...

SO THIS TERM'S PROJECT IS... SPRING CLEANING!

HUH?

DUST!

YOU MAKE THE MESS, YOU CLEAR IT UP! HERE'S A LIST OF JOBS!

GROAN! THAT'S GOING TO TAKE AGES!

JOBS TO DO

ZIP!

COME ON, JANITOR. LET'S HAVE A NICE CUP OF TEA WHILE THEY GET STARTED.

2B

FIRST UP – CLEAN OUT THE KITCHEN CUPBOARDS!

BILLY WHIZZ
THE FASTEST BOY IN THE WORLD!

56 MILLION YEARS AGO. ON A TUESDAY...

SHOOF!

I, YO-BLAB OF THE ZOLGORKS, CLAIM THIS PLANET FOR, ER... WELL, ME, I GUESS!

MINE!

SIR! A METEOR IS ABOUT TO STRIKE THIS PLANET AND DESTROY MOST LIFE!

YIKES! LET'S GET OUT OF HERE, COMPUTER!

BOOM!

I'LL POP BACK LATER.

56 MILLION YEARS LATER. ON A THURSDAY...

SHOOOO OOOF!

I'M BACK, EARTH! MISS ME?

WHO ARE YOU?

DUH! I'M YO-BLAB. THIS IS MY PLANET! GET OFF IT!

NO WAY! THIS IS OUR PLANET!

IS NOT!

IS TOO!

THERE'S ONLY ONE WAY TO SORT THIS. I'M CALLING THE GALACTIC SPACE COURT.

SUDDENLY...

WHO DARES SUMMON THE GALACTIC SPACE COURT?

ME! YO-BLAB!

THESE LOSERS WON'T GET OFF MY PLANET!

IT'S OURS!

LET ME CHECK THE CENTRAL REGISTRY...

YOU'RE IN FOR IT NOW!

RIGHT. I'M BACK!

YO-BLAB DID CLAIM EARTH 56 MILLION YEARS AGO...

SEE?!

...SO THE CLAIM IS NOW LAPSED. YOU CAN CLAIM AGAIN IF YOU WANT.

I'LL PUT IN A CLAIM!

WHAT?!

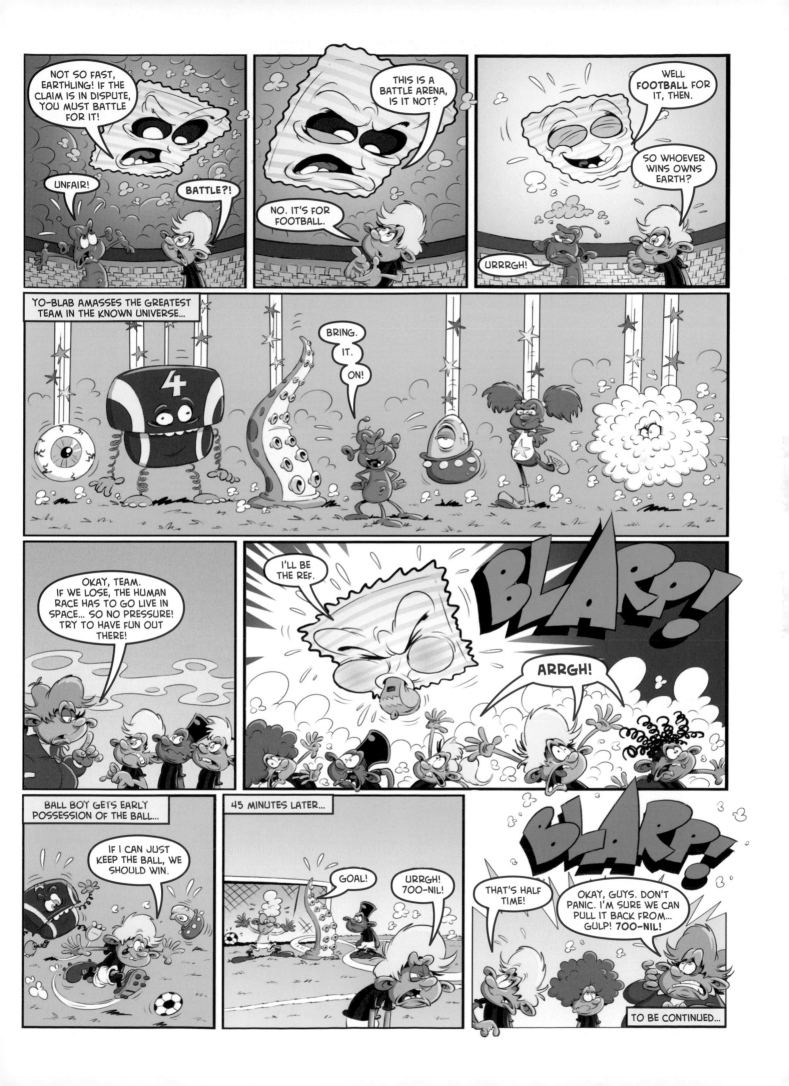

TRICKY DICKY'S
SCHOOL OF PRANKS!

THE NAME'S DICKY! TRICKY DICKY! LICENSED TO PRANK!

YOU'LL NEED:
- JELLY
- A GLASS
- A STRAW

LESSON 1 APRIL FOOLS!

1 First, with the help of an adult, make the jelly following the instructions on the packet.

2

Put your straw in the empty glass.

3 Fill the glass with the jelly mixture and put it in the fridge to set.

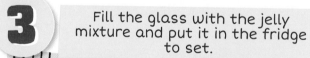

4 Offer your victim a nice, cool drink.

WHEN LITTLE ERIC EATS A BANANA, HE BECOMES...

BANANAMAN

IN GLOOM DOOM!

SPRING HAS SPRUNG! BUT CAN YOU GUESS WHO'S BEEN SPRUNG FROM JAIL?

I'M DYING TO FIND OUT WHO IT IS, BUT I HAVE A MUCH MORE URGENT PROBLEM RIGHT NOW!

WHAT HAVE I DONE WITH MY OTHER BOOT?

YES! WHAT INDEED? I HOPE HE HASN'T LOST IT AND I HOPE DR GLOOM HASN'T FOUND IT AND I HOPE HE ISN'T GOING TO EXTRACT BANANAMAN'S DNA FROM A TOENAIL FRAGMENT, THEN USE IT TO CREATE AN EVIL BANANA-CLONE! – ED

OOH...THAT'S A GOOD IDEA! I'M GOING TO DO THAT!

OOPS! – ED

EVIL DR GLOOM WORKS TIRELESSLY FOR NEARLY 20 MINUTES...

WITH AN EVIL BANANAMAN BY MY SIDE I'LL BE ABLE TO TAKE OVER BEANOTOWN!

BUT...

STRANGE. I'VE MIXED RANDOM STUFF TOGETHER AND THROWN THE BOOT IN...

...BUT IT DIDN'T MAKE AN EVIL BANANAMAN!

AH-CHOO!

AH-CHOO!

OOPS! I APPEAR TO HAVE MADE SOME SORT OF BANANAMAN VIRUS!

AH-CHOO!

AH-CHOO!

HA-HA! IT'S GIVEN ME ALL HIS SUPER POWERS! I'M GOING TO TELL EVERYONE THIS IS WHAT I MEANT TO DO!

FAZOOM!

MEANWHILE...

WHERE'S MY BOOT?

HERE'S A BOOT FOR YOU! HA-HA!

BOOF!

SEE WHAT I DID THERE?!

HAVE WE MET? YOU REMIND ME OF, WELL... TWO PEOPLE ACTUALLY - AND ONE OF THEM IS ME!

OH, YOU'VE MET ME BEFORE... IN YOUR NIGHTMARES!

THAT'S GOOD TOO! I SHOULD WRITE THAT DOWN!

WAIT! YOU'RE DR GLOOM!

NUMSKULLS

The little guys that live in your head! Everybody has them!

THERE'S A LOT GOING ON IN EDD'S HEAD...

IT'S SPRING AND TIME TO...

...KEEP THE WINTER COAT ON FOR A BIT LONGER!

IN EDD'S HEAD, HIS BRAINY IS PLEASED IT'S SPRING...

THANK GOODNESS WINTER IS OVER! I GET SEASONALLY AFFECTED!

WHAT DOES THAT MEAN?

THE DARK AND COLD MAKE ME GRUMPY!

EVERY SEASON MAKES YOU GRUMPY!

NO! I'M ONLY GRUMPY IN WINTER!

IN SUMMER I'M A JOLLY LITTLE FELLOW.

PEACE AND LOVE TO ALL!

DOES THIS SEASONALLY AFFECTED THING AFFECT MEMORY TOO?

NO IT DOESN'T! NOW WINTER'S OVER WATCH HOW LOVELY I BECOME!!!

AT SCHOOL...

SIMMER DOWN, CLASS. WE'RE HAVING A SURPRISE HISTORY TEST.

PHEW! HISTORY. WE'RE AWESOME AT HISTORY!

HISTORY'S THE ONE WITH ALL THE NUMBERS, RIGHT?

THAT'S MATHS.

I KNOW! I'M NOT AN IDIOT!!!

ER... I MEAN THAT'S LOVELY. HAVE SOME CHEESECAKE!

NOW LET'S TAKE A LOOK AT THE FIRST QUESTION.

WHY DID THE ROMANS BUILD STRAIGHT ROADS?

IF ONLY THERE WAS A WAY TO REMEMBER THINGS.

LOOK IN THE MEMORY?

I KNOW THAT!

SPLAT!

I MEAN, HAVING TROUBLE EATING THAT CAKE? LET ME HELP.

IN THE MEMORY...

THIS IS IMPOSSIBLE! HOW'S ANYONE SUPPOSED TO FIND ANYTHING IN HERE?

MAYBE IF WE...

SMASH!

...HEY!

GOOD JOB THAT WAS JUST A MEMORY OF EATING TOAST!

I THINK MAYBE IT'S STILL WINTER. I'VE BEEN HIDING IT WELL, BUT I'M ACTUALLY A BIT GRUMPY!

FOUND IT! THEY BUILT STRAIGHT ROADS BECAUSE A STRAIGHT LINE IS THE SHORTEST DISTANCE!

PHEW!

EDD STARTS TO WRITE THE ANSWER TO THE FIRST QUESTION...

TIME'S UP!

I'M GOING TO BED. WAKE ME UP IF SUMMER EVER GETS HERE.

CALAMITY JAMES

THE UNLUCKIEST BOY IN THE WORLD!

THIS ARTICLE SAYS WHEN SPRING ARRIVES YOU'RE MEANT TO SPRING CLEAN YOUR HOUSE. MUMSIE WILL BE DEAD CHUFFED IF WE DO THAT FOR HER.

'OUR HOUSE IS BETTER THAN THE JONESES'

HOUSE PROUD WEEKLY

AND SO...

I'LL GET THAT COBWEB FIRST.

IT'S SPRING. LET'S CLEAN. BY B. TIDY

GRRR! THAT TOOK ME HOURS TO BUILD!

CRUNCH!

ARRGH! IT'S GOT MY NOSE!

KNOW YOUR SPIDERS

OUTSIDE...

A LITTLE BIT OF WATER WILL SHIFT THE DIRT FROM THE WINDOW.

OOPS! THERE WAS A BRUSH IN THE BUCKET!

SMASH!

HOW TO GLUE A WINDOW TOGETHER

BACK INSIDE...

A DROP OF POLISH AND A GOOD DUSTING WILL SOON SORT THAT VASE OUT!

UH-OH!

SLIP!

AAARGH!

CRASH!

OUCH!

I'LL JUST GIVE THE PLACE A GOOD VACUUM TO FRESHEN IT UP.

CLICK!

VACUUM DAILY

ALIENS STOLE MY VACUUM!

I MUST HAVE HAD IT ON BLOW INSTEAD OF SUCK!

FIXO

FIZZY MILK

WHOOSH!

RIP!

FIZZY MILK

BETTER CHANGE IT!

£100000

COUGH!

WHIRR!

CLICK!

MEGA SUCK!

BUT...

OH CRIKEY! OUR GOOD COUCH!

RIIIP!

WHAT ON EARTH ARE YOU DOING, JAMES?

JUST SOME SPRING CLEANING, MUMSIE!

RUB! POLISH! GLEAM!

TRICKY DICKY'S
SCHOOL OF PRANKS!

THE NAME'S DICKY! TRICKY DICKY! LICENSED TO PRANK!

YOU'LL NEED:
- A BOILED EGG
- CHOCOLATE
- A CHOCOLATE EGG

LESSON 2 EASTER EGG SURPRISE!

1 With an adult's help, melt your chocolate in a bowl over a saucepan of water.

2 I'M AN EGGS-PERT AT THIS

Once it's melted, remove the shell from the boiled egg and completely cover it in chocolate. Leave it to dry.

3 Carefully unwrap the foil around a real easter egg and use it to cover your fake one.

HYUK-HYUK!

4 Leave your fake chocolate egg out for your victim. They'll get an un-eggs-pected Easter surprise!

ARRGH! IT'S A REAL EGG!

THIS PRANK REALLY CRACKS ME UP!

THE ADVENTURES OF BEANOTOWN'S MENACE HOUNDS!

A LONG, LONG TIME AGO, IN A FAR AWAY PLACE...

QUITE A ~~LONG~~, LONG TIME AGO, IN A FAR AWAY PLACE... FAIRLY

~~QUITE A LONG, LONG TIME AGO, IN A FAR AWAY PLACE...~~ ~~FAIRLY~~

TWO DAYS AGO IN BEANOTOWN... JUST BEFORE TEA TIME...

CALAMITY JAMES

THE UNLUCKIEST BOY IN THE WORLD!

DENNIS & GNASHER

THE WORLD'S WILDEST BOY... AND HIS BEST FRIEND!

GOOD MORNING, MY REASON FOR LIVING! IT'S A LOVELY DAY!

REALLY?!

OH YES! IT'S...

...SPLUTTER! SNIFF! IT'S SUMMER! ATCHOO! WHAT'S HAPPENING TO ME?!

LOOKS LIKE YOU HAVE ALLERGIES!

URGH! SPLUTTER! I DON'T GET HAY FEVER!

YOU DO NOW. ALLERGIES CAN START AT ANY TIME!

BY STUFFING GRASS INTO MY JUMPER I'VE MADE MYSELF LOOK LIKE A SCARECROW!

GET AWAY FROM ME!

THIS MUST BE WHAT IT'S LIKE FOR VAMPIRES WHEN PEOPLE WEAR GARLIC!

I'M SURE IT'S EXACTLY THE SAME.

THIS IS THE END FOR ME. I'LL HAVE TO LOCK MYSELF AWAY FROM THE POLLEN...

OR TAKE A TABLET.

...I'LL BE LIKE RAPUNZEL WITHOUT THE HAIR!

HEY, IT'S SUMMER! LET'S GO TO THE BEACH!

I'M GOING TO BED. I'M SICK.

THERE'S MONEY FOR ICE CREAM ON THE KITCHEN WINDOWSILL!

SHOVE!

SO...

I'M GONNA DIG THE BIGGEST HOLE A KID'S EVER DUG! I'VE BROUGHT DAD'S SPADE!

MEANWHILE, WALTER WATCHES FROM THE DUNES...

HMPH! THERE HE IS! WHO BRINGS A GARDEN SPADE TO THE BEACH? WHO DOES THAT?!

WHAT ELSE DO WE HAVE? BEANOTOWN'S YOGA AND MEDITATION CLASS? THEY'RE PROBABLY TRYING TO CONNECT WITH NATURE, OR SOMETHING.

QUIET PLEASE

WHAT ELSE IS THERE?

A GIANT OCTOPUS...

AN OLD SUBMARINE...

WAIT! I'VE HAD AN IDEA!

BILLY WHIZZ
THE FASTEST BOY IN THE WORLD!

THE BASH STREET KIDS

THE CLASS EVERY TEACHER DREADS...

WAHOO! YIPPEE!

SOMEONE SOUNDS HAPPY!

RUMBLE!

WELL, IT IS THE LAST DAY OF SCHOOL!

BUMP!

OOF! WATCH IT, SIR!

THE SUMMER HOLIDAY! MY FAVOURITE TIME OF YEAR! I WON'T SEE THOSE PESKY KIDS FOR WEEKS!

ZOOM!

AH, THIS IS THE LIFE! A DAY AT THE BEACH, RELAXING IN THE SUN.

THINK I'LL HAVE A SNOOZE FIRST...

YAWN!

A QUICK NAP LATER...

I FEEL BETTER AFTER THAT.

WAIT! WHAT?!

HELLO, SIR! THANKS FOR LETTING US BURY YOU IN THE SAND!

I DIDN'T LET YOU – I WAS ASLEEP!

NOW GET ME OUT OF HERE!

SURE THING! WE'LL DIG YOU OUT AS SOON AS WE'VE FOUND WILFRID'S PET CRAB!

THE ADVENTURES OF BEANOTOWN'S MENACE HOUNDS!

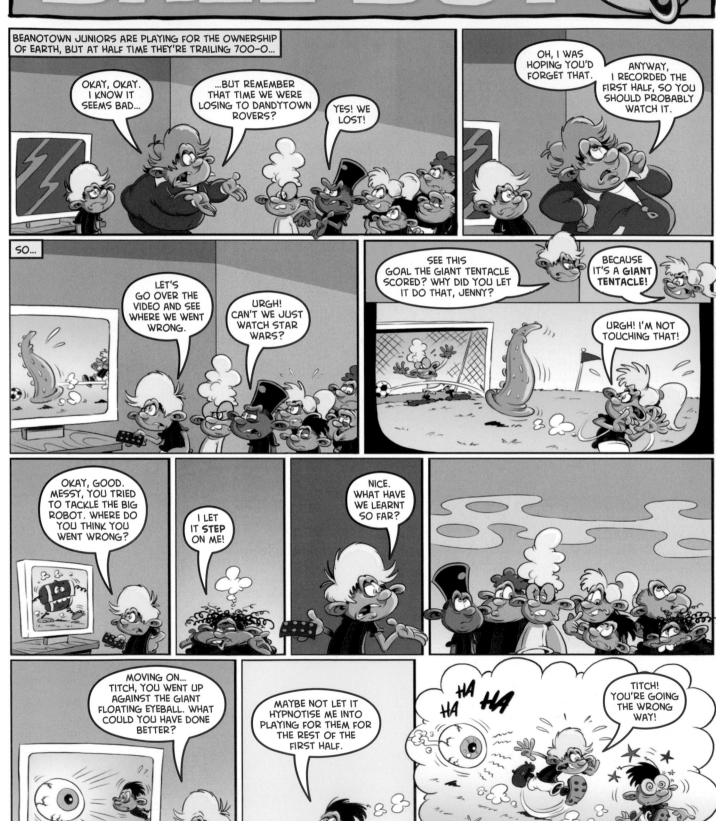

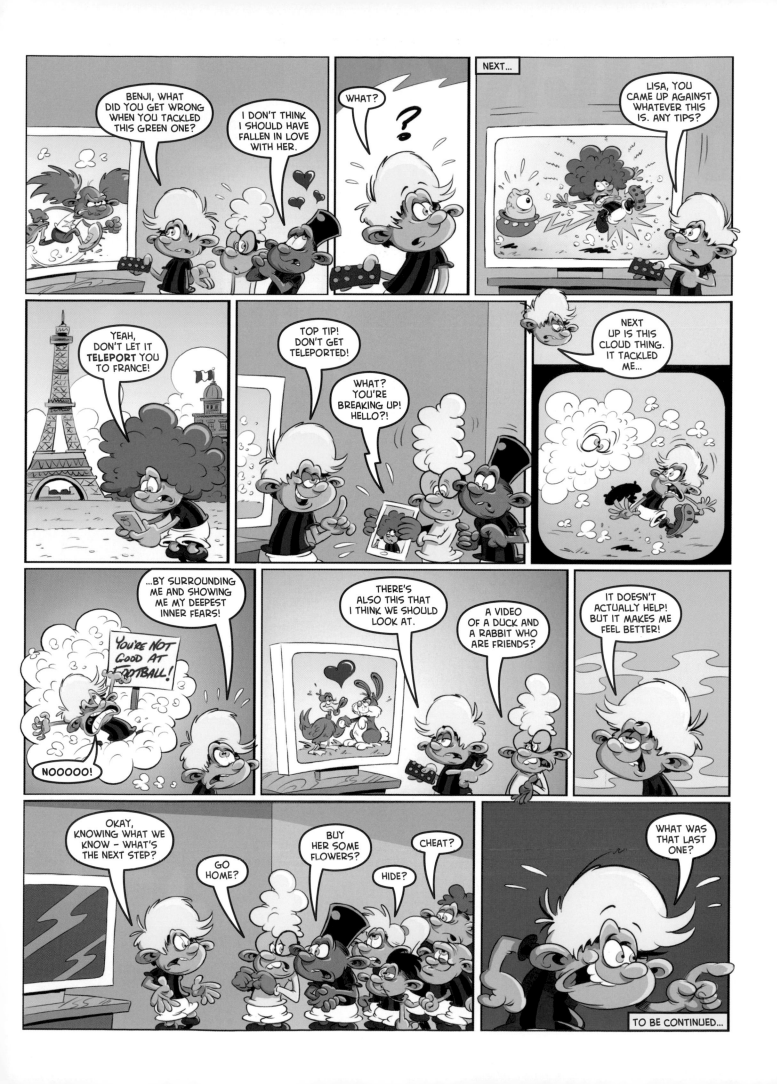

TRICKY DICKY'S
SCHOOL OF PRANKS!

THE NAME'S DICKY! TRICKY DICKY! LICENSED TO PRANK!

YOU'LL NEED:
- ICE TRAY
- MENTOS
- COLA

LESSON 3 A COOL DRINK!

1 Drop the Mentos into your ice tray.

2 Fill the tray with water then put it in the freezer to harden.

3 On a hot day, offer a friend a cool glass of cola. Put the ice cubes in the glass, give your friend the drink and wait.

PHEW! I'D LOVE A COOL DRINK!

COMING RIGHT UP, MIKEY...

4 Eventually the ice will melt and their drink will erupt like lava!

SHRIEK! IT'S ALIVE!

MINNIE THE MINX

SHE'S TOUGHER THAN ALL THE BOYS...

WELL, THIS HAS BEEN GREAT! A NICE, PEACEFUL AFTERNOON ALL TO OURSELVES.

BLISS!

BUT IT'S THE LAST AFTERNOON WE'LL GET, BECAUSE ANY MINUTE NOW...

THE SUMMER HOLIDAYS START HERE! WAHOO!

LOB!

...THAT HAPPENS.

SO! WHAT ARE WE DOING? SHALL WE GO OUT? CAN WE HAVE CHIPS? LET'S PLAY VIDEOGAMES!

WAIT, NO! LET'S GO AWAY!

SO WHERE ARE WE GOING ON HOLIDAY THIS YEAR? A THEME PARK? A REALLY BIG THEME PARK?

HAVE I GOT A SURPRISE FOR YOU...

...TA-DA!

HUH? I CAN'T SEE THE SURPRISE, DAD – THOSE RUCKSACKS ARE IN THE WAY!

THEY ARE THE SURPRISE – WE'RE GOING ON A CAMPING HOLIDAY!

WHAT?!

IT'S A CHANCE TO BOND AS A FAMILY AND TO BE AT ONE WITH NATURE!

I'D RATHER BE AT ONE WITH A MASSIVE THEME PARK!

NONSENSE! COME ON, MINNIE – FREEDOM AND ADVENTURE AWAIT!

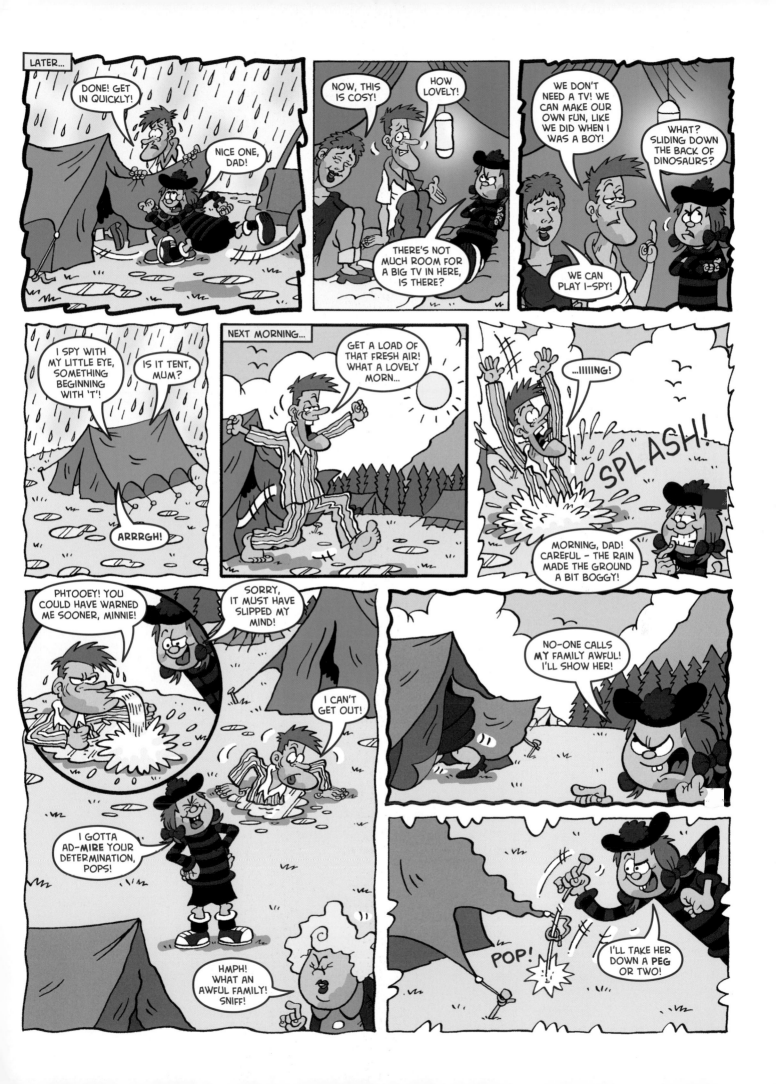

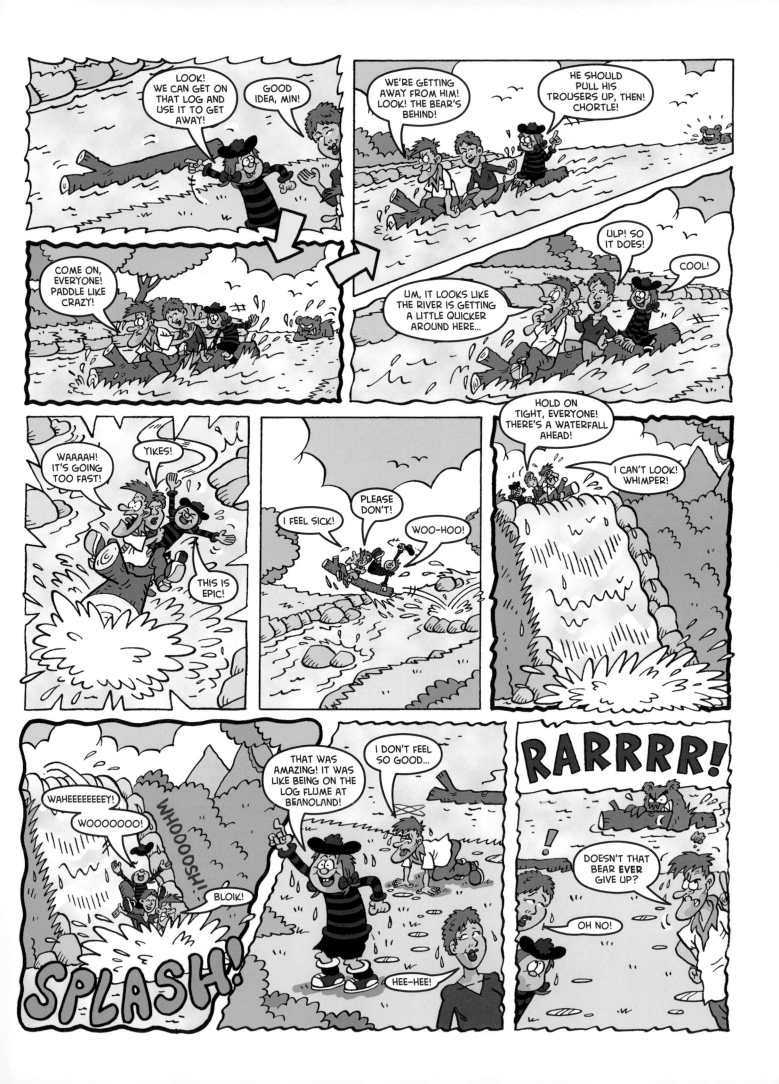

WHEN LITTLE ERIC EATS A BANANA, HE BECOMES...

BANANAMAN

VERSUS THE WEATHERMAN!

IT'S A WINTER OF DISCONTENT IN BEANOTOWN... AND IT SHOULD BE SUMMER! THE FREEZING WEATHER'S CAUSING A REAL PROBLEM FOR BANANAMAN...

GULP! THIS UNSEASONAL WEATHER HAS STOPPED THE BANANA DELIVERIES FROM GETTING THROUGH. THERE ARE NO 'NANAS ANYWHERE! HOW CAN I MAINTAIN MY AMAZING SUPERPOWERS?

A FRUIT SHOP
NO BANANAS!

THE FRUIT SHOP NEXT DOOR
BANANAS - SOLD OUT!!

ANOTHER FRUIT SHOP?
TOTAL BANANA SHORTAGE!!!

SWOOP!

I'LL HAVE TO RELY ON MY EMERGENCY SUPPLIES!

BUT...

OH DEAR! THEY DON'T APPEAR TO BE RIPE JUST YET!

THE ADVENTURES OF BEANOTOWN'S MENACE HOUNDS!

TRICKY DICKY'S
SCHOOL OF PRANKS!

THE NAME'S DICKY! TRICKY DICKY! LICENSED TO PRANK!

YOU'LL NEED:
- A TOILET ROLL
- SCISSORS
- A GLOW STICK

LESSON 4
TRICKY HALLOWEEN!

1 With the help of an adult, cut evil-looking eyeholes out of your toilet roll.

2

Snap the glowsticks and shake to activate them, then stick inside the toilet rolls and secure with tape.

3 Place your toilet rolls in hedges, trees and bushes.

4 Watch as people freak out when they see glowing eyes peering at them!

I WANT MY MUMMY!

BILLY WHIZZ
THE FASTEST BOY IN THE WORLD!

ALFIE'S UPSET BECAUSE HE WANTS TO BE A WIZARD, BUT HE CAN'T DO SPELLS.

WAAAH!

I COULD HELP HIM WITH SOME SUPER-SPEEDY TRICKS.

BACK IN A NANO-SECOND, ALFIE. SEE IF YOU CAN TURN THAT FROG INTO A BEAUTIFUL PRINCESS.

OKAY, BILLY. ABRA-DABRA...

FAZOOOOM!

THIS DUMMY SHOULD ATTRACT MORE CUSTOMERS...

...HUH?!

I'LL BRING IT BACK IN A SECOND!

FAIRY SHOP

WHOOOOOOOOOSH!

BUT BILLY CAN'T SEE WHERE HE'S GOING...

OUCH! MAYBE IT'S NOT A GOOD IDEA!

BLAM!

BACK HOME...

ZOOOOOOM!

TRY AGAIN, ALFIE. MAKE THE LITTLE TOY CAR GROW REALLY BIG!

WHILE I GO UPSTAIRS TO GET THE BIGGER ONE!

BUT BILLY TRIPS DOWN THE STAIRS...

THUD!

ARRGH!!

SMASH!

THIRD TIME LUCKY, ALFIE. TURN THAT FLOWER INTO AN ICE CREAM!

ABRA-DABRA!

CAN'T SEE!

THAT'S THE MAGIC FLASH, ALFIE.

DAZZLE!

NOW TO RUN TO THE SHOP BEFORE ALFIE'S EYES GO BACK TO NORMAL!

ONE WHIZZ-SPEED TRIP TO THE SHOP LATER...

I DID IT!

THAT'S WHAT YOU CALL REAL BILLY WHIZZ-ARDRY! CHUCKLE!

CALAMITY JAMES

THE UNLUCKIEST BOY IN THE WORLD!

NUMSKULLS

The Little guys that Live in your head! Everybody has them!

THERE'S A LOT GOING ON IN EDD'S HEAD...

IT'S AUTUMN. SLOWLY THE GREENS OF SUMMER GIVE WAY TO ORANGE AND BROWN AS THE LEAVES FALL FROM THE TREES...

AHH...

FOR THOSE WITH HAY FEVER IT MARKS AN END TO SNEEZES AND SORE EYES AS THE AIR BECOMES CRISP AND CLEAR...

AHH...

THE SEASON ALSO BRINGS WITH IT HALLOWEEN...

TRICK OR TREAT?

HOW ADORABLE!

ARRRRGH!

WHAT'S UP?

HI, RADAR. I'VE JUST REALISED IT'S NEARLY HALLOWEEN. I'M GOING TO TURN AND LOOK AT YOU NOW...

ARRGH!

RELAX! IT'S ME!

PHEW!

ARRRGH!

PHEW!

HA-HA-HA! I COULD DO THIS ALL DAY!

OH, YOU'RE SO FUNNY!

THAT RADAR THINKS HE'S FUNNY, SCARING ME LIKE THAT. I NEED TO GET HIM BACK!

I KNOW! I'LL USE EDD'S IMAGINATION TO CREATE SOMETHING! TEE-HEE!

SO, ER... SCARY THING. BIG, SCARY THING. REALLY BIG! AND...

...ENTER!

GRRRRRRA!!!

AAARRRRGH.!!

WHAT HAVE I DONE?!

THE EAR DEPARTMENT...

KNOCK! KNOCK! KNOCK!

ALL RIGHT! IT'S ACTUALLY OPEN, YOU KNOW!

GRRRA!

HA-HA! I SCARED YOU!

NOW SAVE ME!

ARRGH!

SO IT'S EATEN US. WAS IT WORTH IT?

TOTALLY.

BALL BOY

HAVING OPTED FOR THE TACTIC OF CHEATING, BALL BOY AND CO. ARE CONFIDENT THEY CAN COME BACK FROM 700 – NIL DOWN...

OKAY, GUYS. GET OUT THERE AND SCORE 701 GOALS!

PLAY LIKE THE PLANET DEPENDS ON IT!

BUT IT DOES!

WHILE YOU EARTHLING LOSERS HAVE BEEN DISCUSSING A FUTILE COMEBACK, I HAVE DESIGNED A TEAM KIT! NOW WE CAN DEFEAT YOU IN STYLE!

TIME TO FOOTBALL SOME MORE!

BLARP!

MEANWHILE, IN FRANCE...

FIRST, I NEED THE TOILET. THEN I NEED SOMEONE WHO KNOWS HOW TO REVERSE TELEPORTATION!

BALL BOY HAS MANAGED TO GET CLOSE TO THE OPPOSITION'S GOAL...

SOMEONE STOP HIM!

BALL BOY SHOOTS...

NOOOOO!

I SCORED!

OFFSIDE!

WASN'T!

WAS SO!

I WILL REVIEW THE FOOTAGE AND CHECK YOUR PRIMITIVE RULE BOOK FOR THE OFFSIDE RULE!

HALF AN HOUR LATER...

MY INTELLIGENCE IS THE GREATEST IN THE UNIVERSE... BUT I JUST DON'T UNDERSTAND YOUR OFFSIDE RULE! I'M GOING TO LET THE EARTHLINGS HAVE THE GOAL!

WE ONLY NEED ANOTHER 700 TO WIN!

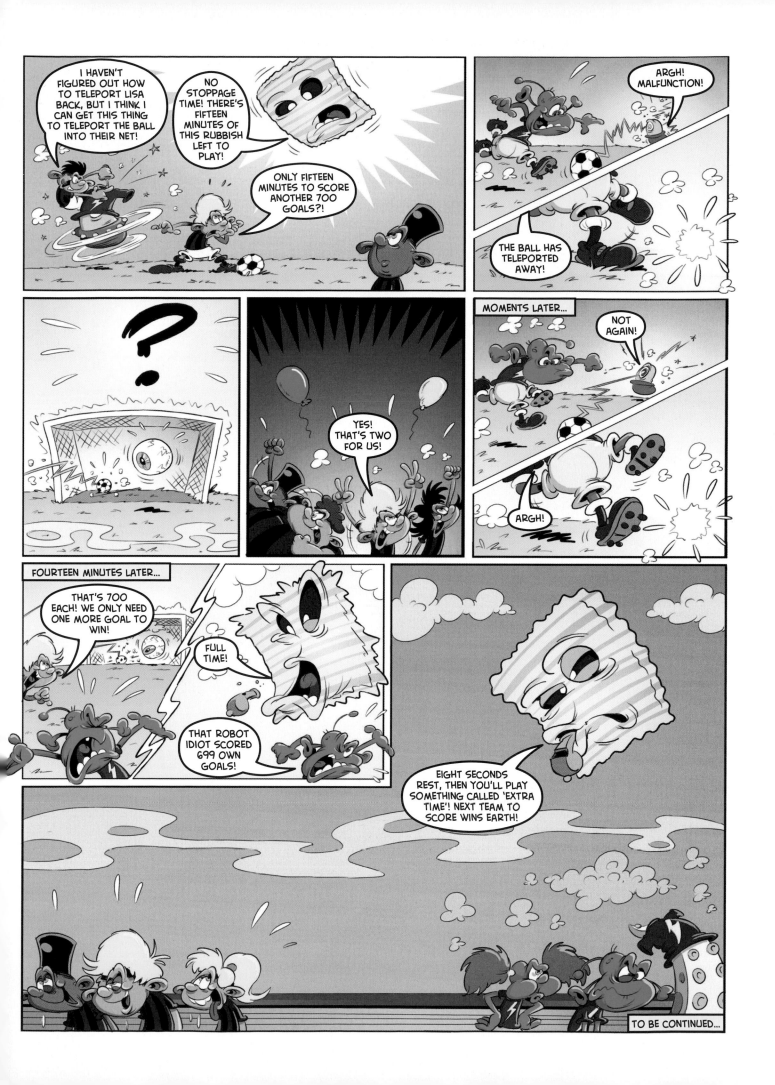

DENNIS & GNASHER

THE WORLD'S WILDEST BOY... AND HIS BEST FRIEND!

IT'S WINDY OUT TODAY, DENNIS.

IS IT? BY THE WAY, IF I SOUNDED LIKE I'M NOT INTERESTED... IT'S BECAUSE I'M NOT INTERESTED.

DAD?!

HNNNHHH.

DAD DID TRY TO SAY MORE THAN 'HNNNHHH' BUT HE'S A GROWN-UP SO WE COULDN'T BE BOTHERED TO FIND OUT WHAT HE WAS TRYING TO SAY.

HA-HA-HA-HA-HA!

ARE YOU PLANNING TO KEEP THIS UP FOR LONG?

WELL...

...HA-HA-HA!

I KNEW WE SHOULD HAVE GOT A GOLDFISH INSTEAD OF KIDS.

20 MINUTES LATER...

YEAH, OKAY. THAT'S ME DONE.

ABOUT TIME, TOO. I WAS GETTING FED UP.

HA-HA-HA!

LOOKS LIKE IT'S MUM'S TURN NOW.

IT WAS THE WIND!

I NEED TO BRUSH MY HAIR, SO YOU CAN CLEAR UP ALL THE LEAVES THE STORMS HAVE BLOWN OFF THE TREES.

HUH?!

OKAY, I ACCEPT THAT THE WIND MIGHT BE RESPONSIBLE FOR YOUR CRAZY HAIR!

MIGHT BE?!

ONE MORE SMART COMMENT ABOUT MY HAIR AND YOU'RE GROUNDED UNTIL YOU'RE 30!

THINK YOU CAN HANDLE ALL THIS EVERY WEEK?

EPIC LAUGHS!

GENIUS PRANKS!

AMAZING PRIZES!

COMIC ADVENTURES!

MEGA PUZZLES!

...AND LOADS MORE AWESOMENESS!

BEANO
ON SALE EVERY WEDNESDAY!

BEANOTOWN ADVENTURE! in THE ROGUE ONES! PART TWO!

IT IS A DARK TIME FOR THE KIDS. MAYOR BROWN IS BUILDING A DEVICE TO STOP ALL THE FUN IN BEANOTOWN. WHILE TRYING TO PINCH THE PLANS, THE KIDS HAVE BEEN CAPTURED...

YOU ARE ALL OUR PRISONERS.

BORING! YOU ALREADY SAID THAT.

OUTSIDE...

OUR PALS HAVE BEEN CAPTURED.

DISASTER! THIS IS WORSE THAN RELEGATION!

CHOC

WE NEED A PLAN.

A CUNNING ONE.

A SNEAKY ONE.

A REALLY DEVIOUS ONE!

WHAT ARE YOU LOOKING AT ME FOR?

OH, ALL RIGHT. I HAVE AN IDEA OF HOW THEY CAN DODGE OUT OF THIS...

YOU WILL ALL BE SENT TO DETENTION UNTIL WE LAUNCH THE MOON WITH THE BIG NAME YOU DON'T LIKE AND WE END FUN IN BEANOTOWN FOREVER!

THAT'S RUBBISH, WIBBLER.

IT'S WILBUR! WILL YOU GET THAT RIGHT? AND YOU WILL NEVER GET YOUR GRUBBY, GROTTY LITTLE HANDS ON THESE SECRET PLANS.

SECRET PLANS

THEY'RE NOT MUCH OF A SECRET WITH YOU WAVING THEM ABOUT, ARE THEY?

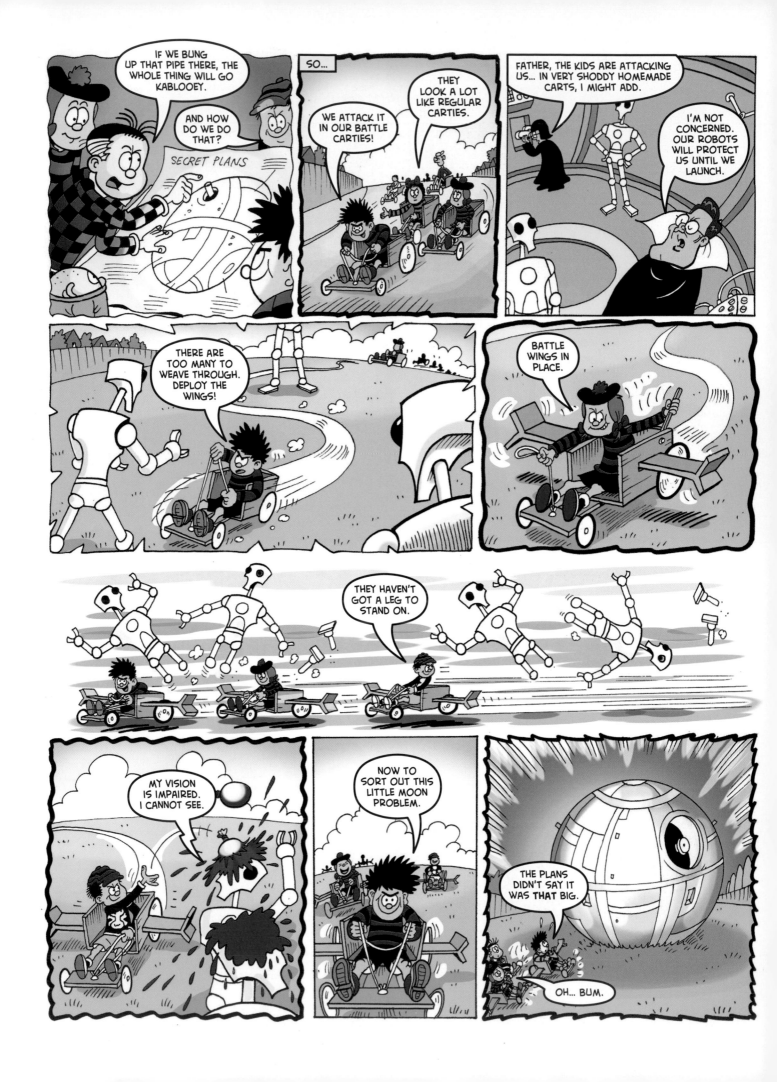

NUMSKULLS

The Little guys that Live in your head! Everybody has them!

THERE'S A LOT GOING ON IN EDD'S HEAD...

IT'S COLD IN EDD'S HOUSE...

BEANO

INSIDE EDD'S HEAD, BRAINY WANTS TO KNOW WHAT'S GOING ON...

WHAT'S GOING ON?

IT'S SIMPLE – EDD'S MUM CAN'T AFFORD TO HAVE THE HEATING ON ALL THE TIME.

YEAH, BUT AUTUMN'S OVER. WHY IS IT NOT GETTING WARMER?

BECAUSE WINTER IS AFTER AUTUMN.

WHAT?!

I THOUGHT IT WENT – AUTUMN, SUMMER, CHRISTMAS, WEDNESDAY, JULY, WINTER!

IT'S NO BIG DEAL. WE JUST NEED TO WRAP UP!

YES! THERE'S NO NEED TO GO OVERBOARD OR TAKE THINGS TOO FAR!

HA-HA! YES! WRAP UP!

SO...

WHAT IS THAT?

I USED EDD'S IMAGINATION TO CREATE A SHEEP THAT LIKES TO KNIT!

HONK!

THAT'S NOT A SHEEP!

WHO ARE YOU? AN ART CRITIC?

IT'S WEIRD AND...

...WAIT. WHERE'S IT GONE?

IT'S GOT ME! ARRRGH!

IT'S GOT RADAR!

URRGH! BET I GET THE BLAME JUST FOR CREATING IT!

HONK! HONK!

HONK!

CALAMITY JAMES

THE UNLUCKIEST BOY IN THE WORLD!

IT'S BEEN POURING FOR DAYS. THIS IS THE WORST WINTER EVER!

LOOK AT THE POOR ANIMALS, ALEX. WE SHOULD BUILD SOMETHING TO HELP THEM STAY WARM AND DRY!

WE'VE NO FENCE NOW BUT IT'S FOR A GOOD CAUSE!

AAARGH! MY THUMB!

MUCH HAMMERING LATER...

THE REMAINS OF THE FENCE.

FINISHED!

WE SHOULD LET THE ANIMALS IN NOW.

BUT THE ANIMALS AREN'T SO KEEN ON THE IDEA...

NO WAY! I'LL TAKE MY CHANCES WITH THE RAIN!

ARE YOU BARKING MAD?!

TIM HAS A BIT OF A BAD TEMPER.

I'M NOT GOING IN THAT THING!

UNGRATEFUL ANIMALS. WHAT MORE COULD THEY NEED?!

HANG ON! WHAT'S THAT NOISE?

CREAK! GROAN!

ARRGH! I FORGOT THE ROOF! IT'S FILLED UP WITH RAIN WATER! GLUG!

GUSH!

THE BASH STREET KIDS

THE CLASS EVERY TEACHER DREADS...

MORNING, EVERYONE!

WHY ARE YOU SO HAPPY, CUTHBERT?

SKIP! SKIP!

TEACHER HAS ASKED ME TO ORGANISE THE BASH STREET CHRISTMAS FAYRE! IT'S BOUND TO GET ME TO THE TOP OF SANTA'S GOOD LIST!

OH NO! I'D FORGOTTEN ABOUT THE GOOD LIST. WE'RE NEVER GOING TO GET ON IT!

NOT UNLESS WE ORGANISE THE FAYRE!

GREAT IDEA, TOOTS!

ON THE DAY OF THE FAYRE...

HELLO!

WHAT ARE YOU LOT DOING HERE?

WE'VE COME TO HELP!

4 CANDLES

CHRISTMAS

WE'LL HAVE EVERYTHING WRAPPED UP IN NO TIME!

BUT I DON'T NEED YOUR HELP!

OF COURSE YOU DO!

WE LOVE CHRISTMAS!

BUT YOU'LL RUIN CHRISTMAS!

SNATCH!

DON'T BE SILLY!

LATER...

WHERE'S CUTHBERT?

HE'S A LITTLE TIED UP! BUT DON'T WORRY, WE'VE ORGANISED EVERYTHING! WE'VE EVEN DECORATED THE HALL!

WISH LIST CHEESE CHEESE CHEESE CHEESE CHEESE

ALTHOUGH PUTTING SMIFFY IN CHARGE WAS PROBABLY A MISTAKE!

HAPPY HALLOWEEN!

SCHOOL HALL

BOYL!! BOYL!!

HE'S FOOTBALL CRAZY!
BALL BOY

BALL BOY AND CO. HAVE MANAGED TO EQUALISE. IT'S EXTRA TIME...

TELEPORTING THE BALL INTO THEIR NET 699 TIMES WAS GENIUS!

I'LL SEE IF I CAN BRING YOU BACK, LISA!

THAT WOULD BE GREAT! DOES ANYONE KNOW HOW TO ASK WHERE THE TOILETS ARE IN FRENCH?

PHWEEP!

GOLDEN GOAL! NEXT TEAM TO SCORE WINS EARTH!

BALL BOY TAKES POSSESSION OF THE BALL...

THAT CLOUD ALIEN HAS LOST THE BALL! IT LOOKS LIKE IT'S STARTING TO QUESTION ITS OWN EXISTENCE!

WHAT'S THE POINT?

WE'VE MANAGED TO TAKE CONTROL OF THE TELEPORTER THING!

I'VE CONFUSED THE GREEN ONE BY GIVING IT SOME FLOWERS!

WHAT IS THIS THING YOU CALL LOVE, HUMANS? THAT ACT OF KINDNESS HAS CAUSED ME TO MALFUNCTION!

AND THE HUGE TENTACLE'S STILL STRUGGLING TO GET ITS SOCKS ON!

LOOK! THE HUGE FLOATING EYEBALL'S GOT SOME ORANGE JUICE IN ITS, ERM... EYE!

ONLY THE ONE DEFENDER TO BEAT!

YOU WON'T GET THROUGH ME, EARTH BOY!

I NEED TO CROSS IT, BUT THERE'S NO-ONE UP FRONT!

TRICKY DICKY'S
SCHOOL OF PRANKS!

THE NAME'S DICKY! TRICKY DICKY! LICENSED TO PRANK!

YOU'LL NEED:
- A LOT OF WRAPPING PAPER
- A LOT OF STICKY TAPE

LESSON 5
THAT'S A WRAP!

1 Wait until your victim is out of the room.

2  Wrap everything in their room in the paper. We mean everything!

DON'T FORGET THE STUFF IN HIS DRAWER!

3 Now tell your victim that you got them something special for being so good this year.

WE'VE GOT A SPECIAL CHRISTMAS SURPRISE JUST FOR YOU, MR THROBB!

4 Then watch as they have to unwrap everything they own!

ARRGH! WHERE IS MY FAVOURITE MUG? ARRGH! MY CAR KEYS!

WHEN LITTLE ERIC EATS A BANANA, HE BECOMES... BANANAMAN

VERSUS **GENERAL BLIGHT!**

WINTER DRAWS ON AND THE THREAT TO BEANOTOWN HAS RISEN TO LEVEL THREE BECAUSE WE'RE RUNNING OUT OF ANNUAL AND IT'S TIME FOR THE BIG SHOWDOWN...

OH, HE'S GOOD! VERY GOOD! BUT NOT AS GOOD AS I SHALL BE...

WHAT'S THAT FIENDISH ARCH-VILLAIN READING?

I CAN'T SEE HOW THIS WILL THREATEN MY AWESOME SUPERPOWERS.

GENERAL JUMBO!

I CAN'T SEE HOW THIS WILL THREATEN MY AWESOME SUPERPOWERS.

WHIRR!

SCOOSH!

ARRRRGH! A WHITEOUT!

DENNIS & GNASHER

THE WORLD'S WILDEST BOY... AND HIS BEST FRIEND!

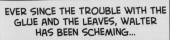
EVER SINCE THE TROUBLE WITH THE GLUE AND THE LEAVES, WALTER HAS BEEN SCHEMING...

...AND PULLING BITS OF DRIED GLUE FROM HIS HAIR...

...AND STRAY LEAVES FROM WHEREVER HE FINDS THEM...

MY LAST, AND SOMEWHAT **MESSY**, ENCOUNTER WITH DENNIS TAUGHT ME A VERY IMPORTANT LESSON...

...DENNIS CAN'T RESIST TEMPTATION.

TEMPTATION

SO I AM GOING TO MAKE SURE HE FACES LOTS OF TEMPTATION, ENDS UP ON THE NAUGHTY LIST AND GETS...

...NO PRESENTS AT CHRISTMAS!

MIRROR, MIRROR, ON THE WALL, WHO'S THE CLEVEREST ONE OF ALL?

YOU ARE, WALTER.

MEANWHILE...

I DON'T LIKE THAT ADVERT, GNASHER. SOME PEOPLE MIGHT SEE US AS A LITTLE BIT NAUGHTY.

REMEMBER: NAUGHTY KIDS GET NOTHING AT CHRISTMAS

GNEVER!

TV WILL CHEER US UP.